EXPLORE THE U.S.A.

DISTRICT OF COLUMBIA

Karen Durrie

AV² provides enriched content that supplements and complements this book. Weigl's AV² books strive to create inspired learning and engage young minds in a total learning experience.

Your AV² Media Enhanced books come alive with...

 Audio
Listen to sections of the book read aloud.

 Video
Watch informative video clips.

 Embedded Weblinks
Gain additional information for research.

Try This!
Complete activities and hands-on experiments.

 Key Words
Study vocabulary, and complete a matching word activity.

 Quizzes
Test your knowledge.

 Slide Show
View images and captions, and prepare a presentation.

... and much, much more!

Go to **www.av2books.com**, and enter this book's unique code.

BOOK CODE

F468684

AV² by Weigl brings you media enhanced books that support active learning.

Published by AV² by Weigl
350 5th Avenue, 59th Floor
New York, NY 10118
Website: www.av2books.com   www.weigl.com

Library of Congress Cataloging-in-Publication Data

Durrie, Karen.
 District of Columbia / Karen Durrie.
    p. cm. -- (Explore the U.S.A.)
 Includes bibliographical references and index.
 ISBN 978-1-61913-337-2 (hard cover : alk. paper)
 1. Washington (D.C.)--Juvenile literature. I. Title.
 F194.3.D87 2012
 975.3--dc23
                              2012014760

Printed in the United States of America in North Mankato, Minnesota
1 2 3 4 5 6 7 8 9 16 15 14 13 12

052012
WEP040512

Project Coordinator: Karen Durrie
Art Director: Terry Paulhus

Weigl acknowledges Getty Images as the primary image supplier for this title.

DISTRICT OF COLUMBIA

Contents

3

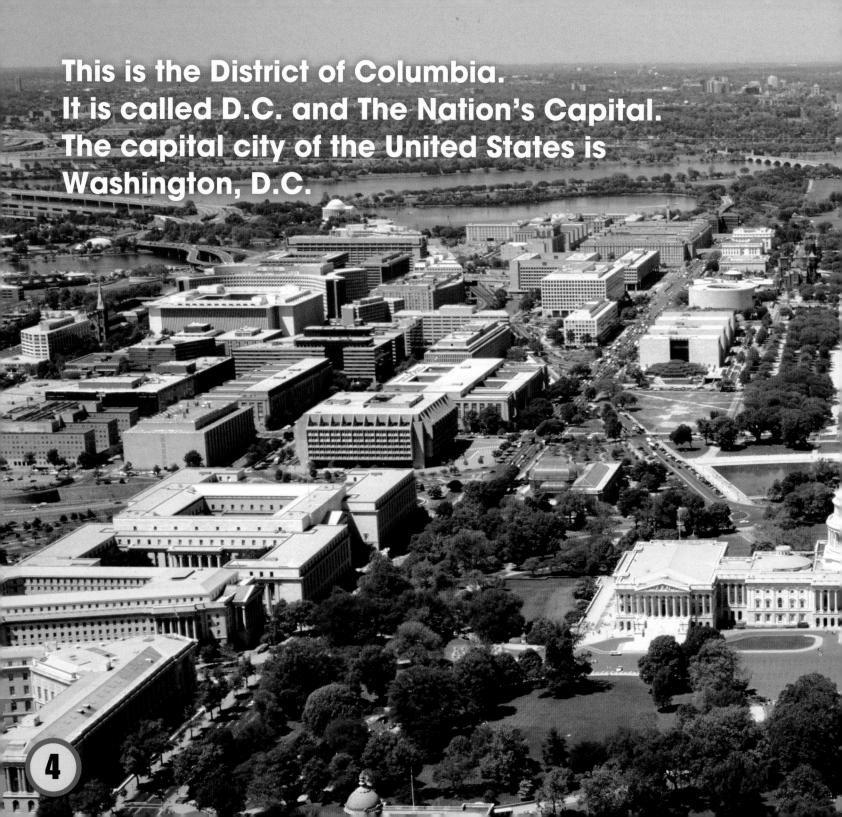

This is the District of Columbia.
It is called D.C. and The Nation's Capital.
The capital city of the United States is
Washington, D.C.

This is the shape of the
District of Columbia.
It is in the east part
of the United States.

Where is the District of Columbia?

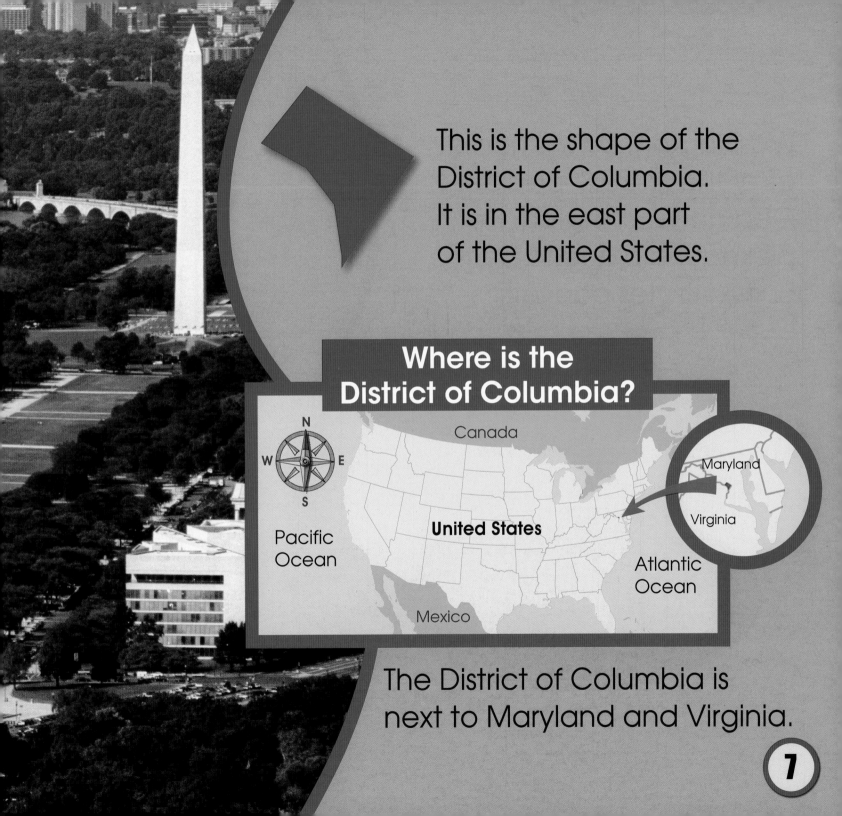

Canada

Maryland

Virginia

United States

Pacific
Ocean

Atlantic
Ocean

Mexico

The District of Columbia is
next to Maryland and Virginia.

Washington, D.C. is named after the first U.S. president, George Washington. He picked this place to be the United States capital.

The United States government is in the District of Columbia.

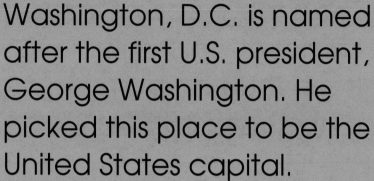

The American Beauty rose is the district flower. It has 50 petals and a nice smell.

The district seal has a building, a woman, and a statue of George Washington.

The building on the seal is the Capitol building.

This is the flag of the District of Columbia. It has three red stars and two red stripes.

There was a contest to design the District of Columbia flag.

The wood thrush is the district bird. A wood thrush can sing two notes at the same time.

The wood thrush makes a sound like a flute.

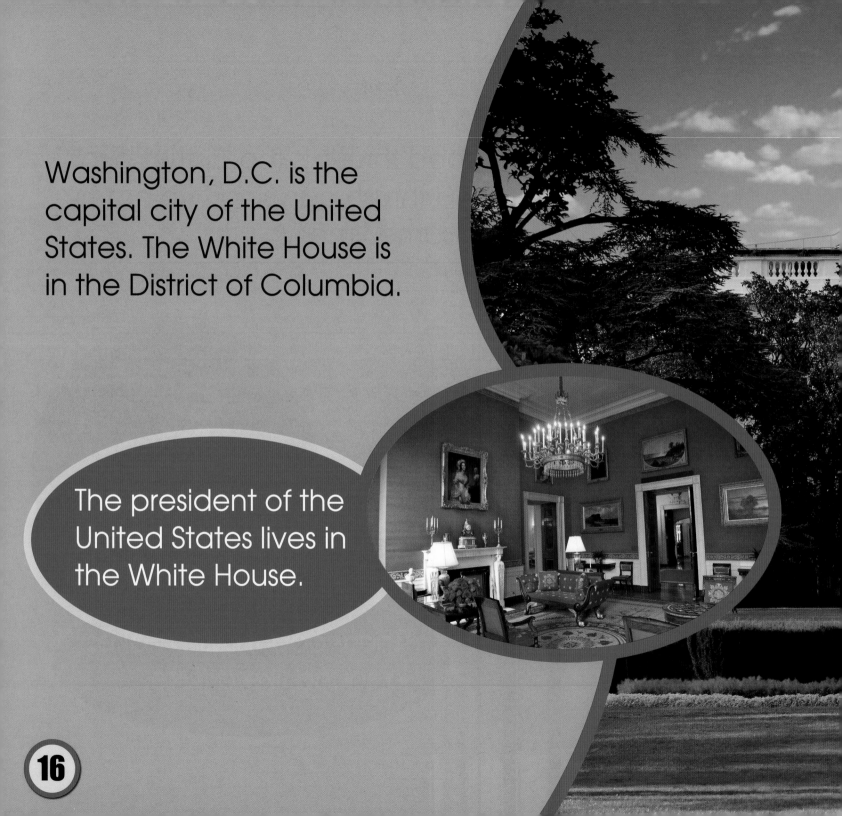

Washington, D.C. is the capital city of the United States. The White House is in the District of Columbia.

The president of the United States lives in the White House.

Airplanes and airplane parts are made in the District of Columbia. Many different airplanes for the military are made there.

The president of the United States travels in an airplane called Air Force One.

There are many famous buildings and statues in the District of Columbia. More than 15 million people from all over the world come to D.C. to see the sights.

DISTRICT OF COLUMBIA FACTS

These pages provide detailed information that expands on the interesting facts found in the book. These pages are intended to be used by adults as a learning support to help young readers round out their knowledge of each state in the *Explore the U.S.A.* series.

Pages 4–5

The District of Columbia is not a state but a federal district that was created to be the seat of the United States government. Federal districts are under direct control of their governments and are not part of any state or capital. The District of Columbia is also called Washington, D.C., or simply D.C.

Pages 6–7

The United States Congress created the District of Columbia on July 17, 1790. The District of Columbia is surrounded by the states of Virginia and Maryland. It is about 68 square miles (176 square kilometers). Washington, D.C. is located in the middle of the eastern seaboard, about 90 miles (145 kilometers) inland from the Atlantic Ocean. More than 618,000 people live in Washington, D.C.

Pages 8–9

The Residence Act, passed by Congress on July 16, 1790, stated that the site of the new nation's capital would be along the Potomac River. George Washington chose the exact location for the new city. Maryland and Virginia each transferred portions of their states for the new city, although the land given by Virginia was returned in 1846.

Pages 10–11

The great seal of the District of Columbia shows Lady Justice hanging a wreath on a statue of George Washington. Lady Justice represents the justice system. The D.C. motto, *Justitia Omnibus*, is written on the seal. It is Latin for "Justice for All." The U.S. Capitol building is in the background. The seal also depicts a train, a rising sun, and water. It was created in 1871.

KEY WORDS

Research has shown that as much as 65 percent of all written material published in English is made up of 300 words. These 300 words cannot be taught using pictures or learned by sounding them out. They must be recognized by sight. This book contains 48 common sight words to help young readers improve their reading fluency and comprehension. This book also teaches young readers several important content words, such as proper nouns. These words are paired with pictures to aid in learning and improve understanding.

Page	Sight Words First Appearance
4	and, city, is, it, of, the, this
7	in, next, part, to, where
8	after, be, first, he, named, place
11	a, has, on
12	there, three, two, was
15	at, can, like, makes, same, sound, time
16	lives
19	an, are, different, for, made, many
20	all, come, from, more, over, people, see, than, world

Page	Content Words First Appearance
4	District of Columbia, Nation's Capital, United States, Washington, D.C.
7	Maryland, shape, Virginia
8	capital, George Washington, government, president
11	American Beauty, building, Capitol Building, eagle, flower, petals, rose, seal, smell, statue, woman
12	contest, flag, stars, stripes
15	bird, flute, notes, wood thrush
16	president, White House
19	Air Force One, airplanes, military
20	sights

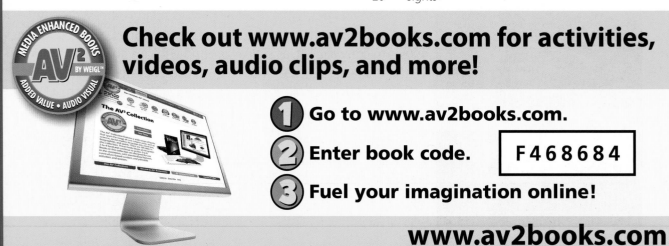

Check out www.av2books.com for activities, videos, audio clips, and more!

1 Go to www.av2books.com.

2 Enter book code. **F468684**

3 Fuel your imagination online!

www.av2books.com